The Country Kitchen

GIFTS
HOMEMADE

Anne Chapman

The Country Kitchen

GIFTS
HOMEMADE

Anne Chapman

HARLAXTON
PUBLISHING

Front and back of jacket: Homemade gifts laid out ready for presentation. Left to right: toffee apples (p.36), gingerbread men (p.41), cumquat brandy, mint vinegar (p.26), orange liqueur (p.46), thyme vinegar, cold pressed olive oil, candied cumquats (p.30), toffees (p.36), Valentine cookies (p.39), rosemary vinegar, brandied prunes (p.45), plum sauce (p.23) and tarragon vinegar (p.26).

Front and back endpapers: An old-fashioned country kitchen with the preparation for a spicy fruit cake in the foreground. The wood-burning stove is wonderful for long, slow cooking.

Page 2: A delicious olive paste to spread on crusty bread or toast fingers. Give a jar away with a copy of the recipe.

 COOK'S NOTES: Standard spoon measurements are used in all recipes.
All spoon measurements are level.

All ovens should be preheated to the specified temperature.

Fresh herbs are used unless otherwise stated. If they are unavailable, use half the quantity of dried herbs. Use freshly ground black pepper whenever pepper is used. Add salt and pepper to taste. Use all-purpose flour unless otherwise stated.

Published by Harlaxton Publishing Ltd
2 Avenue Road, Grantham, Lincolnshire, NG31 6TA, United Kingdom.
A Member of the Weldon International Group of Companies.

First published in 1992.
Reprinted in 1993.

© Copyright Harlaxton Publishing Ltd
© Copyright design Harlaxton Publishing Ltd

Publishing Manager: Robin Burgess
Project Coordinator: Barbara Beckett
Designer & Illustrator : Barbara Beckett
Photographer: Ray Jarratt
Editor in United Kingdom: Alison Leach
Typeset in United Kingdom: Seller's, Grantham
Produced in Singapore by Imago

British Library Cataloguing-in-Publication data.
A catalogue record for this book is available from the British Library.
Title: Country Kitchen Series: Gifts-Homemade
ISBN:1 85837 002 7

CONTENTS

COUNTRY KITCHEN GIFTS

WE ALL LOVE to give presents and to receive them. A prettily wrapped, mysterious package is always exciting. If it is a homemade gift, it is all the more exceptional. The thoughtfulness and the time spent on creating it go toward making the recipient feel very special.

Nearly everyone appreciates good food. It is not only one of the necessities of life but one of the great delights. When you give an edible gift you give something to be savored. Your friends will think of you every time they bite into the orange marmalade or exclaim over the subtle flavor of your homemade country-style pâté.

Dare I add that homemade gifts cost less than bought ones. A full bottle of fruit liqueur can be made with half a bottle of the cheapest brandy or gin and some fruit and sugar–not very expensive, and so delicious. Make pickles, chutneys and fruit liqueur's when there is a glut of plums, cherries or oranges in the markets. Plan to make presents all through the year, taking advantage of gluts and making use of windfalls, and you will always have edible gifts. Most chutneys, fruit preserves and liqueur's improve with age.

Some of the recipes in this collection are for edibles that should be consumed soon after they are made, such as the pear and rum sauce (to serve with Christmas plum pudding) and the country-style pâté. Others are for special occasions: a delicious fruit Christmas cake, Easter cookies and St Valentine cookies. You will find plenty of ideas among the recipes for presents: gingerbread men and coconut macaroons for children, walnut cake for your father-in-law, cherries in brandy for your best friend. There are curry pastes for making authentic indian curries; olive paste to take as a gift for a barbecue lunch, delicious on crusty bread while you wait for the food to cook; pineapple marmalade to put under the Christmas tree as a thank-you gift for the next-door neighbors; and edible gifts from a country garden, such as a bouquet of herbs, aromatic herbs for the barbecue and herbal teas.

I hope you enjoy using these recipes as much as I have. Many were given to me in the first place. Recipes themselves make a lovely gift accompanied by a sample of the recipe's end-product. It is fascinating to think how recipes get recycled from friend to friend, often changed slightly before being passed on. What joy we are giving to one another!

Bon appetit!

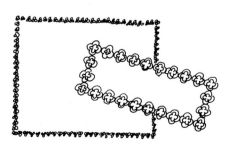

Tarragon vinegar and other herb vinegars make especially good gifts. Always be on the lookout for attractive bottles. A ribbon and a nice label make the bottles so much more festive.

HOMEMADE PACKAGING

Containers

Making gifts through the year requires some planning ahead. Containers are an important consideration. Recycle all your bottles and jars, especially finely shaped ones. I find I don't buy many things in containers, as I make most of my own food, so I have trained 'non-cooking' friends and family to give me their bottles and jars. This arrangement works successfully because they all know the containers will come back full of country goodness.

Wash bottles and jars very thoroughly and take off the labels before storing. Stubborn labels can be removed with lighter fluid. When you bring the bottles and jars out for use, wash and rinse them again and sterilize them just before they are needed. The easiest method of sterilizing glass containers is to place them in a slow oven 225°F for 20 minutes. Use jars with plastic screw tops; metal shouldn't be used, as it corrodes.

Keep attractive boxes, coffee cans, cake tins and any sort of attractive container that could be recycled. Paste paper over boxes and tins that are a great shape but have ugly advertising on them. Try painting them. Explore antique markets for cheap old glass bottles and jars, pieces of china, interesting old tins or boxes.

Buy good preserving jars with screw tops and bottles with metal-wired glass lids and rubber rings. They last for ever and look attractive on the kitchen shelves.

Small straw baskets are not expensive to buy and make perfect containers for many gifts, such as Easter eggs and gingerbread men. For extra special gifts, it is worth while buying new boxes; they come in all shapes and sizes covered with decorative paper.

Paper

All presents are enhanced by being presented in an attractive way. It is not necessary to buy expensive paper. Brown paper, cellophane and tissue paper, even newspaper and white wallpaper, can look attractive. Cut out with pinking shears for a change. Paint a bright pattern in poster paints over newspaper or brown paper –or ask your children to paint it for you.

I make potato prints on newspaper and brown paper. It's easy to do. Simply cut a potato in half and draw the pattern you want on the surface. Cut away about 1/4 inch from the pattern, leaving it raised. Mix some poster paint with water in a saucer and dip the potato in. Have the paper ready, and print away. Black and gold look handsome on brown paper or red and green print up well for Christmas. If you are unsure of your skills in drawing a pattern, trace one off something you like. Print cards and labels with the same pattern as all patterns in books look like labels.

Save all the gift wrapping paper and cards you receive and recycle them. Cut out some of the best designs and paste them down on a gift as a label or card. I save ribbons as well and press them with an iron to remove the creases. I have a ribbon basket with what looks like hundreds of different colors and widths. I love to rummage in it for harmonious colors of ribbon, paper and gift. Kitchen string looks great.

Dish cloths are an appropriate wrapping for an edible gift and look very attractive.

Use gift wrapping paper to cover the lids of recycled jars as well. I also save fabric for jam and chutney covers; an old skirt of Liberty print has covered many a jar. Choose a satin ribbon to tie the cover in place. I glue the paper or

Cumberland sauce is wonderful with all cold meats. It enhances any simple meal.

fabric onto the lid so it does not come off after the bottle is opened. Harmonize colors of the preserves with the lid and ribbon and final wrapping paper. Add a few flowers or herbs to the ribbon bow for a country-style flourish.

Labels

Labels are a most important element. Never forget to label a jar as soon as you seal it up. I am usually in a hurry or tired at that stage, so I write up a rough one on masking tape and stick it on the jar. When I am more relaxed I 'dress' the jars and bottles, making attractive covers for the lids and writing out the labels. One of my friends buys pretty stickers with angels on them and Beatrix Potter characters for the jars of her gifts for children. Attractive labels are fairly cheap to buy, but you can easily make them. Write the name of the contents, the date it was made and perhaps the recommended 'eat-by' date. It is thoughtful to present a recipe to make with presents like plum sauce or Thai red curry paste.

FROM A COUNTRY GARDEN

Bouquet of Herbs

What could be nicer to give than a fresh herbal bouquet? Arranged attractively so that all the subtlety of the individual species can be seen, it is a delight to the eye as well as the senses. You can use it now or later, fresh or dried.

The varying textures and colors of herbs look most attractive together. They need a strong design element to hold the bouquet together–a ribbon, a paper doily or cellophane paper. Try to have some herb flowers in the bouquet if possible. Study the textures and arrange leaves so that they stand out against each other but still harmonize.

Tiny herb bouquets in front of each place setting make a very attractive table decoration. Encourage your guests to take them home.

Tussie Mussie

The *tussie mussie*, or nosegay, is another pretty bouquet, but of herbs and cottage garden flowers, dried or fresh. *Tussie mussies* were carried even up to the Victorian era to disguise the dreadful smell in the towns and cities and as a protection from disease. Aromatic herbs such as rosemary, thyme and lavender were the first disinfectants. Here are a few ideas for *tussie mussies*:

ROSE SALAD BOUQUET
Start with a few roses in bud, some sage, basil, thyme, violets, some long strands of lemon peel and surround with watercress. Cut a hole in the centre of a doily, poke the stem through it and tie the whole bouquet together, trimming the ends. Rose petals and violets are delicious in a salad.

FRESH SALAD BOUQUET
Put together basil, nasturtium flowers and leaves, romaine leaves, some mint and sorrel and surround them with spinach leaves. Tie and cut the stalks evenly. Wrap the bouquet in waxed paper and string.

DRIED TUSSIE MUSSIE
This bouquet starts off fresh; but all the herbs dry very well, so they can be used for a long time to eat from as well as to perfume the room.

Gather together thyme, sage, lavender in flower, rosemary and oregano, and surround them with bay leaves. Arrange the leaves so they contrast each other. Trim the stalks. If you are giving the bouquet to a special friend, use a lace handkerchief instead of a doily to contain it and tie with a pastel satin ribbon. No need to cut a hole in the handkerchief!

BOUQUET GARNI
Make a pretty bunch of the classic herbs used to flavor soups and casseroles. They can be picked out of the bouquet as needed. Bay leaves, thyme, rosemary, tarragon, fennel stalks – put together a large bouquet of these herbs, dried or fresh. Surround them with lemon and orange peel and plants that don't dry successfully, such as tiny carrots, parsley, and celery tops, so that they can be used fresh.

The classic bouquet garni comprises bay leaves, thyme and parsley, but the other herbs can be substituted. Fennel and lemon peel taste good with fish dishes; rosemary and tarragon are added for chicken and lamb; orange peel for meat dishes.

Wrap in brown paper cut with pinking shears, and tie with thick gardening string.

A bouquet of herbs makes a thoughtful gift to a gourmet cook.

Pot of Herbs

A very refreshing spicy tea mixture which looks as attractive as it tastes. it is fun to experiment and create original blends.

A living plant is a wonderful gift. It can bring pleasure for years as a visual and a culinary delight. I make up containers of mixed herbs and vegetables for my friends as the seedlings and cuttings in spring. They are then transferred to the gift pots. It takes several months for the plants to grow.

Put seedlings in terracotta pots, the older the better. I like the warm patina of moss. Always use a good light potting compost, and remember to water frequently, as pots dry out quickly. Give them liquid fertilizer every 2 weeks while they are growing. Label them if necessary.

Some potting suggestions: cherry tomatoes surrounded by basil; parsley, chives and sorrel; rosemary, salad burnet and parsley; basil, bronze fennel and cilantro; spinach and cherry tomatoes; sage, oregano and tarragon; mar-joram and savory; chives and sage; a small bay tree with thyme as a ground cover; a lemon tree surrounded with basil.

Some herbs and plants are better in their own pots, as they tend to overwhelm their companions. Lemon grass, and strawberries are among those best on their own.

Gift wrap the pot base with brown paper, cellophane or newspaper and tie with string or satin ribbon. You may need to put some plastic under the pot first to stop the moisture from dripping through. Add a card with a description of the plants; giving some information about how to care for them and perhaps also providing a recipe or two for their use.

Aromatic Barbecue Mixture

Fresh herbs thrown into the barbecue while the meat is cooking can enhance the flavor of the meat besides adding an extra pungency to stir the taste buds while you wait. The oils from the fresh herbs give out a powerful scent. Once the herbs are dried, they are rather like potpourri and should be thrown on the barbecue just a bit before eating, as their aroma does not last very long.

A bowl of aromatic herbs, fresh or dried, makes a lovely, thoughtful gift. Make up mixtures of any of the following herbs: rosemary, thyme, marjoram, fennel stalks, oregano, garlic, lavender, sage, savory, and bay leaves. Other aromatics that will mix with these herbs are orange and lemon peel; eucalyptus leaves and pine needles. Add some spices; juniper berries, sticks of cinnamon, star anise, whole cloves, coriander seeds and fennel seeds. Put the mixture into bowls, screw-top jars or cellophane bags tied with a bow.

Herbal Teas

Herbal teas are a pleasant change from coffee and China or Indian tea. They can also be beneficial to the health. They make a lovely present as a box of dried teas or individual sachets wrapped in cheesecloth. Your friends will think of you every time they sip the tea.

As a rule, herbal teas are composed of individual herbs, but a mixture or the addition of spices can be very interesting. Among the herbs you can dry and use for teas are seeds from dill and fennel, lemon grass, lemon verbena, thyme, camomile, rosemary, rose hip, peppermint and sage.

Make herbal tea the same way as you make Indian tea, by infusing a spoonful in a teapot for 5 to 10 minutes.

Spicy Tea Mixture

1 1/2   *cups Darjeeling tea leaves*
3   *star anise, crushed*
2   *sticks cinnamon, crushed*
  Peel of half a lemon, dried and chopped
3   *cloves, crushed*
6   *peppercorns, crushed*

Mix all the ingredients together and place in an airtight box or tin. On a label describe the contents. This tea is ideal to refresh the spirits on a cold winter afternoon.

APPETIZERS

Rosemary Walnuts

A very tasty treat that looks good decorated with fresh rosemary.

1 1/2 tablespoons butter
1 1/2 tablespoons olive oil
3   cups shelled walnuts
4   tablespoons chopped rosemary
1/4   teaspoon cayenne
1   teaspoon salt

Melt the butter and oil in a saucepan and add the walnuts and rosemary. Sauté until the walnuts are golden-brown. Add the cayenne and salt and cook for 2 more minutes.

Take the walnuts and rosemary out with a slotted spoon and drain on paper towels. When cool, store in a screw-top jar or cellophane bag; add some fresh sprigs of rosemary. Label and wrap a ribbon around the container. Tie a branch of rosemary in with the bow.

Spicy Cashew Nuts

Delicious with pre-dinner drinks. The nuts would look attractive presented in a glass dish – not an expensive item if bought second-hand.

2   cups raw cashew nuts
2   tablespoons butter
1   teaspoon salt
1   teaspoon curry powder or garam masala
1   teaspoon cumin seeds, ground
1/4   teaspoon cayenne

Walnut Paste

I first tasted this walnut paste in sandwich fingers at a party where the hostess is famous for her party cooking. The sandwiches were the hit of the evening.

4 1/2 cups walnut pieces
2   tablespoons freshly grated
       parmesan cheese
1   teaspoon salt
1   teaspoon ground coriander
1   teaspoon ground cumin
2   cloves garlic, crushed
2   teaspoons balsamic vinegar
2   tablespoons virgin olive oil

Heat the walnut pieces in the oven and grind them in a food processor while still warm. Add the cheese, salt, spices, garlic, vinegar and half the oil. Blend until smooth. Put into sterilized jars and pour a thin layer of oil on top to seal. Label and attach serving ideas.

Use for sandwich fingers and individual brioches, fill celery sticks 2 inches long, or spread on toast.

Opposite: I call walnut paste the gourmet's peanut butter. It makes delicious sandwiches–no need for butter.

Melt the butter in a saucepan and sauté the cashew nuts until they are golden. Stir in the seasonings and cook for a few more minutes. Take out the cashews with a slotted spoon; drain on paper towels. When cool, store in a clean screw-top jar. Decorate the lid and label.

Olive Paste

A delicious paste to spread on bread or toast fingers instead of butter and serve with drinks before dinner. It is very easy to make. A good gift for a friend who doesn't cook.

1	*pound black olives*
2	*teaspoons finely chopped thyme*
1	*bay leaf, crushed and broken up*
2	*teaspoons salt*
2	*teaspoons white wine vinegar*
2	*teaspoons extra virgin olive oil*

Pit the olives. Put all the ingredients in a food processor and blend until smooth. Store in sterilized jars. Pour a thin layer of oil on top to seal.

Olives

If you are lucky enough to have access to an olive tree, olives are very rewarding to preserve. They can then be stored in oil with many different flavors. Olives bought preserved in brine can be drained and stored in any of the ways outlined below. A jar of attractively presented olives makes a wonderful gift.

TO PRESERVE FRESH BLACK OLIVES
Choose firm olives and prick them all over with a needle. Put them on a large cane tray, sprinkle well with enough salt to coat all the olives. If you don't have a cane tray, tape a couple of layers of cheesecloth over a large tray so that there is room for the liquid to run away.

It will take up to 4 days for the olives to lose their bitterness. Shake them three times a day. You may need to add more salt towards the end. Put the olives into clean, sterilized jars and cover with olive oil. See the following recipes for interesting aromatic flavors to add:

GARLIC & THYME

1   pound preserved olives
10 cloves garlic, cut lengthwise into strips
    Thyme
    Bay leaves
    Olive oil

Cut an incision with a sharp knife along the length of each olive. Pack olives into jars in layers alternating with garlic and stalks of thyme. Add one bay leaf per jar. Cover with olive oil.

CHILI

1   pound preserved olives
1   tablespoon red chili peppers
    Olive oil

Chop the red chilies finely and scatter onto the olives as they are placed in the jars. Cover with olive oil.

BAY LEAVES & OREGANO

1   pound preserved olives
4   bay leaves, broken up
1   tablespoon oregano
    A piece of lemon peel
    Olive oil

Combine the olives, herbs and lemon peel in sterilized jars and pour olive oil over them.

 COOK'S NOTES: Nuts and olives make delicious and filling appetizers. Added herbs or spices enhance their flavors.

Easter Eggs

These marbled eggs are extremely beautiful, each one different from the next. An attractive way to give them as a gift is to line a basket with leaves and place the eggs in it.

12 eggs, free range if possible
    Onion skins, brown, red and white
12 pieces of cheesecloth, 6 inches square

Wrap the eggs in onion skins so that you get all the different colors against the egg. Wrap a piece of cheesecloth around each egg to hold the onion skins in place. Secure with string.

Put the eggs in a saucepan and cover with water. Slowly bring to a boil and simmer for 12 minutes. Remove from heat and let the eggs sit in the water until they are cool. Unwrap and refrigerate.

Cooking Kit for Kids

The art of fine cooking is a wonderful possession, something that can give you joy every day of your life. It is never too early to teach children to cook. The chemistry will fascinate them –the knowledge that they actually created biscuits from flour, butter and water. And of course, they learn early that ones own cooking always tastes best.

Put together a first cook's kit for a curious child. Into a large mixing bowl put an apron, pastry cutters, plastic measuring spoons and jugs, one large and one small knife, a wooden spoon, spatula and a rolling pin. Include a list of kitchen safety rules and a few simple recipes. Some easy recipes to start with are fruit and nut fudge (page 35), coconut chocolate (page 38), coconut macaroons (page 39), and ginger nuts (page 41).

Opposite: Thai red curry paste is a much appreciated present, as it takes the hard work out of Thai cooking.

Thai Red Curry Paste

This recipe makes 3 small jars of paste. Give them to friends with the recipe, handwritten, for Thai country-style beef which follows. The paste lasts for months and saves the effort of making it whenever you feel like cooking Thai food. Keep it in a sealed jar in the refrigerator. The more dried chilies you add, the redder the paste will be; but if you remove the seeds, it is safe to increase the chilies without increasing the heat. Shrimp paste is available at Oriental food stores.

1	teaspoon peppercorns
2	teaspoons coriander seeds, roasted
2	teaspoons cumin seeds, roasted
1	teaspoon ground nutmeg
1	teaspoon ground mace
1	tablespoon chopped dried red chilies
2	tablespoons shrimp paste (kapee)
1/2	cup onions chopped
1/2	cup garlic chopped
1/2	cup chopped lemon grass or lemon peel
1	tablespoon chopped cilantro
	Zest of 1 lime or lemon
1	tablespoon salt

Grind together the peppercorns, coriander and cumin seeds, nutmeg, mace and chilies. Put this powder into a food processor with the remaining ingredients and blend to a smooth paste. When packing the paste into the jars, check carefully that there are no air bubbles. Dispel any bubbles with a spatula.

Madras curry paste (Madrasi masala) is a rich, spicy blend perfect for this broiled masala chicken.

Four Spices (Quatre Épices)

This is a French spice mixture used for flavoring pies, sausages, meatloaves and pâtés. It is a fragrant blend of pepper, cloves, nutmeg and ginger. By blending your own, you obtain an extra freshness. You will never again want to buy the ready–made commercial product after tasting this. I have added a recipe to give with a jar of *quatre épices*.

2 1/2 tablespoons peppercorns
1   tablespoon whole cloves
1   tablespoon freshly grated nutmeg
1   tablespoon ground ginger

Blend the peppercorns and cloves in a food mill or clean coffee grinder. Mix with the nutmeg and ginger and store.

Masala Chicken

Spicy broiled chicken to eat with rice and a minty salad.

1   chicken, cut into 10 pieces
1 1/2 tablespoons madras curry paste
      (see opposite)
1   cup yogurt
4   red chilies, chopped
1   teaspoon salt
      Juice of half a lemon

Take the skin and fat off the chicken pieces. Combine all the other ingredients in a bowl and mix well. Coat the chicken pieces with the marinade and let them marinate for at least an hour or preferably overnight in the refrigerator.

Preheat the broiler. Broil the chicken pieces for 10 to 15 minutes on one side. Turn them over and cook for a further 10 to 15 minutes. Serve straight away. Serves 4-6.

Madras Curry Paste
(Madrasi Masala)

This fragrant blend of spices preserved in oil takes all the hard work out of Indian cooking once you have a store of the paste. It will last up to 6 months stored in an airtight bottle in the refrigerator. I recommend grinding your own spices to make an especially fresh mixture to start with.

1	cup coriander seeds, ground
1	tablespoon cumin seeds, ground
1	tablespoon black peppercorns, ground
1	tablespoon mustard seeds, ground
1	tablespoon turmeric
1	tablespoon salt
1	teaspoon ground cloves
2	teaspoons crushed and chopped garlic
2	teaspoons finely grated ginger root
1 1/2	teaspoons white wine vinegar
1/2	cup vegetable oil

Combine all the ingredients except the oil in a bowl and mix into a smooth paste. Heat the oil in a pan and put the paste in. Stirring constantly, cook until the spices are cooked and the oil separates. Bottle in sterilized jars.

Country-Style Pâté

Keep this hearty pâté refrigerated for several days to allow it to mature.

6	slices bacon
1	pound chicken livers
1	pound lean ground pork
1	egg, beaten
2	cups soft bread crumbs
2	tablespoons brandy
2	cloves garlic, crushed
1	teaspoon chopped thyme
8	juniper berries, crushed
2	teaspoons black pepper
1	teaspoon salt
1/2	teaspoon four spices (see left)

Cut the rind from the bacon slices and line a terrine dish with them, letting the ends overhang on one side–they will be used to cover the top of the pâté. Clean the chicken livers and grind them. In a bowl, combine the ground liver with all the other ingredients and mix well. Put the mixture into the terrine dish and fold the bacon ends over the top. Cover with the lid of the terrine or foil. Put the terrine into a baking dish and add 3/4 inch of hot water to the dish. Place in a preheated oven at 350°F for 1 1/2 hours. Cool and refrigerate.

Thai Country-Style Beef

2	pounds stewing steak
2	cups coconut milk
3	tablespoons red curry paste (page 17)
2	cups water
2	sticks lemon grass, 2 3/4 inches long
1	teaspoon salt
3	red chilies, chopped

Take all the fat off the beef and cut into bite-size pieces. Put the coconut milk in a saucepan and bring to a boil. Add the curry paste; stir well for 5 minutes. Add the meat, coating all the pieces with the sauce. Stir for 5 minutes, then add all the other ingredients. Bring to a boil, cover, and simmer slowly for 1 1/2 hours or until the beef is tender. Add more hot water if the sauce begins to dry out. Serves 6.

SAUCES

Rhubarb & Ginger Sauce

This sauce has a most attractive color. It is ideal with pork and can be eaten warm or cold with all cold meats. I find that friends who do not cook very much appreciate this sauce.

1	cup white wine vinegar
1	cup sugar
	Zest and juice of 2 oranges
1	red chili
1	teaspoon allspice berries
1	teaspoon mustard seeds
1/2	teaspoon cinnamon
6	stalks rhubarb, washed, trimmed and cut into 2 inch pieces
	Zest of 1 lemon
1	tablespoon chopped ginger root
1/2	cup golden raisins
1	teaspoon salt

Place vinegar, sugar, orange juice, chili, allspice, mustard seeds, cinnamon in a saucepan and bring to a boil. Add rhubarb, with the zest, ginger, golden raisins and salt. Simmer for about 45 minutes or until it thickens slightly. Ladle into warm sterilized jars.

Opposite: I created this sauce when I was given a basket of rhubarb from a friend's country garden. I made a chutney first, which inspired me to make a rhubarb and ginger sauce.

Tomato Sauce

Tomato sauce will keep for months. It is handy to have in ready supply and is a useful gift to take to a barbecue.

2	pounds tomatoes, peeled
2	tablespoons olive oil
1/2	cup onion finely chopped
4	cloves garlic, finely chopped
2	tablespoons finely chopped parsley
2	tablespoons finely chopped basil
	Salt and pepper

Roughly chop the tomatoes. Heat the oil in a large saucepan and add chopped onion. Stir until it is translucent. Add garlic and cook for 1 minute. Add parsley and basil; season to taste. After it has come to a boil, simmer for an hour, stirring occasionally. Remove from the heat and leave to stand for 30 minutes.

Put a couple of basil leaves in each sterilized jar, then pour in the sauce. Top with a thin layer of oil to seal the sauce. Label and store in a dark, cool place.

Cumberland Sauce

This delicious sauce is wonderful with poultry, game and smoked tongue.

2	shallots, finely chopped
4	oranges
2	lemons
2	cups redcurrant jelly
1	tablespoon Dijon mustard
3	tablespoons red wine
2/3	cup Port
	Salt and pepper

Rhubarb & ginger
Sauce

Make plum sauce with windfall plums. I look forward to making a huge potful every summer.

Put the shallots in a pan, cover with cold water and bring to a boil. Simmer for a few minutes and strain. Peel oranges and lemons very thinly with a potato peeler; cut the peel into julienne strips. Blanch them in the same way as the shallots. Melt redcurrant jelly in a heavy pan.

Stir in the mustard, wine, port, shallots and peel. Season with the salt and pepper, simmer for about 20 minutes, until the sauce is fairly thick. It will thicken more as it cools. Bottle and keep in a cool, dark place.

 COOK'S NOTES: Homemade sauces, sweet and savory, make cooking so much faster once the sauces are made, and all you have to do is choose which one will go with the lamb, chicken or dessert of the day.

Pear & Rum Sauce

This is a wonderful accompaniment to the plum pudding at Christmas and makes a nice change from traditional sauces. Of course, it's delicious as well over vanilla ice-cream. Make it the day you are going to eat it. Warn your host you are bringing the sauce for the Christmas pudding!

1	cup dark rum
2	tablespoons brown sugar
6	pears, cored, peeled and chopped
1	cup unsalted butter

Put half the rum and sugar in a saucepan and dissolve the sugar. Add the pears and stew until they are soft. Blend in a food processor.

Melt butter, add purée and remainder of the rum. Heat until it is blended. Store in a suitable container. Heat thoroughly before serving.

Plum Sauce

Plum sauce matures with time, so keep this for 2 months before opening it. It is an old-fashioned sauce and usually made with windfall plums. Any variety of plum can be used, but I usually make sauce with the plums that aren't so nice to eat fresh.

4	pounds plums, pitted
1	cup onions finely chopped
1 1/4	quarts white wine vinegar
1	tablespoon salt
1	cup golden raisins
1/4	teaspoon cayenne
1	teaspoon crushed allspice berries
1	tablespoon grated ginger root
3	cloves garlic, crushed
1 1/2	cups granulated sugar

Put all ingredients into a large saucepan. Bring to a boil, then gently simmer for 1 1/2 hours. Ladle into sterilized jars. The sauce will thicken as it cools. Seal and label.

Mustard

Mustard is generally made from the seeds of black mustard (*Brassica nigra*) and white mustard (*Brassica alba*). If you haven't a food mill, use a coffee grinder to grind the seeds. Put mustard into small sterilized jars or pots and keep for 2 weeks before using. Small white porcelain bowls make a present into a gift.

Bavarian Mustard

This is a mild, sweet and sour mustard perfect for serving with veal sausages, smoked pork or lamb chops.

2	tablespoons black mustard seeds
2	tablespoons white mustard seeds
2	tablespoons grated horseradish, fresh if possible
1	teaspoon salt
1	teaspoon olive oil
3	tablespoons white wine vinegar
1	teaspoon honey

Grind mustard seeds, then put ground seeds in the blender with the other ingredients. Blend to a smooth paste. Bottle and label.

Overleaf: Who could resist a plum pudding as a gift? These puddings are also easy to make.

Tarragon Vinegar

Herb vinegars make a very attractive gift in a nicely shaped bottle. Olive oil bottles are usually a lovely shape to recycle.

1   cup tarragon
1   quart wine vinegar

Put the tarragon in a wide-necked jar and pour vinegar over it. Cover and leave for 2 weeks, shaking the jar every day. Strain the vinegar into sterilized bottles. Add a sprig of tarragon to each bottle.

VARIATIONS: Use the same method for making marjoram, thyme, basil or rosemary vinegars.

Mint Vinegar

Use bottles with fairly wide necks; you may have trouble removing the leaves from a fancy shape. After the vinegar is strained, it can be put into narrow-necked bottles. This vinegar has a nice sharp flavor. I sometimes use it to freshen up a gravy sauce.

2   cups mint leaves
1/2   cup granulated sugar
1 3/4 pints cider vinegar

Combine mint with the sugar in a sterilized bottle. Bring the vinegar to a boil and pour over the sugar and mint. Allow to stand for 10 days, shaking the bottle daily. Strain and bottle again.

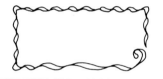

Opposite: This spicy oil is delicious to cook with. It makes a great start to a pasta sauce or provençale chicken.

Country-Style Mustard

White mustard seeds are much stronger in flavor than black. Compare this flavor with the mustard on page 23. The flavors are endlessly fascinating to experiment with.

1   tablespoon black mustard seeds
3   tablespoons white mustard seeds
1   tablespoon finely chopped tarragon
1   tablespoon finely chopped parsley
1   teaspoon salt
1   tablespoon olive oil
3   tablespoons cider vinegar
1   tablespoon honey

Grind mustard seeds in a grinder and put into a blender with the rest of the ingredients. Blend to a smooth paste. Spoon into sterilized jars.

Spicy Oil

Don't use the most expensive extra virgin oil for this hearty oil. A cheaper cold-pressed oil will do very well. Spicy oil is excellent to have by a barbecue for basting meats or vegetables.

3   red chilies
2   cloves garlic
1   teaspoon cumin seeds, ground
1   teaspoon coriander seeds, ground
5   cardamom pods
10   black peppercorns
3   cups olive oil

Put the spices into a sterilized oil bottle and pour the oil over them. Seal and label.

Cold Pressed Olive
Oil
with chilli, bayleaves,
margarin, garlic.

PRESERVES

Spiced Cherries

Spiced cherries are excellent with roast turkey and are traditional on Christmas Day at my home. A jar of spiced cherries makes an extra special gift.

2	*pounds cherries, washed*
2	*cloves*
1	*teaspoon coriander seeds*
1	*tablespoon grated ginger root*
1	*cinnamon stick*
1	*cup granulated sugar*
1 1/2	*cups wine vinegar*

Prick the cherries a few times with a needle. Tie up the spices in a cheesecloth bag. Put the sugar, vinegar and spices into a saucepan and bring to a boil, stirring to dissolve the sugar. Add the cherries and cook gently for 5 to 10 minutes until they are tender. Spoon into sterilized jars, seal and label.

Pickled mushrooms are very handy to have in the store cupboard to enhance a buffet table or take to a picnic.

Pickled Mushrooms

I find pickled mushrooms give an air of luxury to any outdoor occasion, from a simple picnic to the most sophisticated event. They are easy to prepare but are best made from the smallest, most perfect mushrooms you can buy.

1	*pound button mushrooms*
	Salted water
2 1/2	*cups white wine vinegar*
10-12	*peppercorns, cracked*
2 or 3	*bay leaves, broken*
1	*large onion, sliced*
2	*cloves garlic, bruised*
1	*sprig thyme or rosemary*

Trim stems of the mushrooms, place in a large saucepan with salted water to cover and bring to a boil over medium heat. Remove from heat, allow to stand for 5 minutes, then drain and dry the mushrooms on paper towels. Combine the vinegar with the peppercorns, bay leaves, onion, garlic and thyme or rosemary in an enamel saucepan. Bring to a boil, then lower the heat and simmer for 5 minutes. Strain and keep the spiced vinegar hot.

Fill clean, heated jars with the mushrooms, and pour in the spiced vinegar to the rim of each jar. Seal with acid-proof seals, allow to cool, and store in a cool place for 2 to 3 weeks before using.

Apple & Pear Chutney

Chutneys are amongst the homeliest and tastiest gifts you can give. They store well, improving with age, and are infinitely superior to any bought ones.

1 1/2	*cups granulated sugar*
1	*cup white wine vinegar*
2	*teaspoons allspice berries*
1	*tablespoon chopped ginger root*
6	*cloves garlic, crushed*
1	*tablespoon salt*
2	*red chilies*
3	*cups apples, peeled and chopped*
3	*cups pears, peeled and chopped*
2	*tablespoons golden raisins*

Put sugar, vinegar and spices into a saucepan and bring to a boil, stirring to dissolve the sugar. Add the fruits and simmer for 45 minutes; stir from time to time, especially towards the end, in case the mixture catches on the bottom of the saucepan. When it is soft and thickened, it is ready.

Ladle into sterilized jars. Seal and store in dark, cool place. Don't forget to label and date the chutney.

Spiced Prunes

Delicious with roast pork or rare roast beef for a change.

1	*cup wine vinegar*
1	*cup granulated sugar*
1/2	*teaspoon grated nutmeg*
1/2	*teaspoon ground pepper*
1	*red chili*
1	*pound prunes, pitted*
2	*tablespoons brandy*

 COOK'S NOTES: Save all your bottles for storing jams, chutneys and pickles. Recycle pretty material for cloth covers and ribbons. Re-use attractive wrapping paper to cover commercial boxes and coffee cans.

Put the vinegar, sugar and spices in a saucepan and slowly bring to a boil, stirring to dissolve the sugar. Pack the prunes into sterilized jars and pour the syrup over them, making sure to dispel any air bubbles. Pour some brandy into the jars and seal. It is best to let the prunes mature for a few months before opening.

Date & Banana Chutney

Tamarind paste is available in health food and Oriental food stores. To make up the liquid, put 2 teaspoons of paste in a bowl and pour over a cup of boiling water.

1	cup tamarind liquid
1/2	cup brown sugar
1/2	cup wine vinegar
3	red chilies, chopped
1	teaspoon cumin seeds, ground
1	teaspoon cardamom seeds, ground
1	teaspoon salt
1	cup dates, pitted and chopped
3	green bananas, sliced

Put tamarind liquid, sugar, vinegar and spices into a saucepan and bring to a boil, stirring occasionally. Add dates and bananas and gently bring to a boil. Cook, simmering for about 45 minutes or until the liquid is absorbed and the mixture is thick. Stir to prevent the chutney sticking to the base of the saucepan. Pour into sterilized jars and seal.

Glacé Cumquats

This recipe takes 7 days to make. It is well worth the effort and only a little work is needed each day. Keep the syrup as it is delicious poured over ice-creams or fruit salads.

1	pound cumquats
1	tablespoon salt
1	pound granulated sugar
2 1/2	cups water
1/2	cup granulated sugar

Day 1: Wash the cumquats well and prick each about eight times with a needle. Put them into a bowl with the salt and enough water to cover. Soak overnight.
Day 2: Put the cumquats into a saucepan with fresh water to cover and bring to a boil.

Pineapple Marmalade

Marmalades are easy to make and are popular gifts. Bottle in attractive jars, glue pretty material onto the lids and tie with ribbon.

3 1/2	cups pineapple finely chopped
3	lemons, thinly sliced
1 3/4	quarts water
4	pounds granulated sugar

Put the pineapple, lemons and water in a large saucepan and simmer for 1 1/2 to 2 hours or until the fruit is very soft. Add the sugar and stir until it dissolves. Turn the heat up and boil very fast for about 20 minutes or until the setting point is reached. (Test the marmalade to see if it gels on a cold plate.)

Remove from the heat and leave to rest for 15 minutes, spoon into sterilized jars and seal.

VARIATION: Use finely sliced oranges instead of pineapple if you want a more traditional marmalade.

Opposite: Glacé cumquats make a very special gift. They are so delicious it is hard to give them away.

Simmer until they are tender–30 to 50 minutes. Drain and put into the bowl. At the same time, make a syrup with 1 pound sugar and water. When it becomes clear, it is ready. Pour syrup over cumquats and leave to stand overnight.
Day 3: Drain the syrup off the cumquats and put it into a saucepan, adding 1/4 cup sugar. Bring to a boil and, when clear, pour over the cumquats. Leave for 48 hours.
Day 5: Repeat day 3 process.
Day 7: Drain the cumquats, reserving syrup, roll in granulated sugar and place on a wire rack and dry in a very slow oven. Store in an airtight tin or wide-necked bottle.

VARIATION: Instead of drying the cumquats, keep them in the syrup.

Glacé Cumquats

Orange & Chili Marmalade

Here is a jam packed with vitamin C and a very pretty color with the orange and red chilies.

2	pounds oranges, thinly sliced
	Juice and zest of 1 lemon
6	cups water
6	red chilies, whole
4	pounds granulated sugar

Put the oranges, lemon and water into a large saucepan and bring to a boil. Simmer for about 1 1/2 hours or until the oranges are almost tender, add the chilies after 45 minutes.

Add the sugar and stir until it is dissolved. As soon as the marmalade comes to a boil, turn up the heat and cook very fast for about 20 minutes or until the setting point is reached. (Test for the setting point by putting a drop of marmalade onto a very cold plate. If it crinkles when pushed and doesn't run, it is ready).

Take the marmalade from the heat. Leave to stand for 15 minutes to distribute the fruit and then ladle into sterilized jars and seal.

 COOK'S NOTES: Preserve fruit and vegetables when there is a glut in the market and the prices have fallen. Take advantage of windfalls too and watch out for people who don't harvest their fruit–they are often eager to have you pick the fruit for them to save the mess of fallen fruit.

Apple & Rosemary Jelly

The rosemary adds a delicate fragrance to the apply jelly. Crab apples can be used instead or in an apple mixture.

2	pounds apples, peeled and chopped
3	tablespoons rosemary
	Granulated sugar to measure
	Sprigs of rosemary

Put apples and rosemary into a saucepan with just enough water to cover them. Simmer for an hour. Strain the mixture through a jelly bag or a strainer lined with four layers of cheesecloth sitting over a large bowl. It will take 1 or 2 hours to strain. Do not touch the fruit or jelly bag, as this will cloud the jelly.

Measure the juice in a measuring jug as you ladle it into the saucepan. Add equal measures of sugar to the juice. Dissolve sugar in the juice and bring to a rapid boil. Boil until the setting point is reached. Test by dropping a small amount on a cold plate. If it gels, it is ready.

Remove from heat, skim, and immediately pour into sterilized jars. Add a sprig of rosemary to each jar. Seal and label. Do not move the jars until the jelly is firmly set.

 COOK'S NOTES: Never forget to label and date the jars as soon as you have filled them. Clean the outside of the jars and inside the neck before sealing, and make sure there are no air pockets. Dispel with a spatula to remove risk of bacteria developing.

SWEETS & SWEETMEATS

Candied Peel

All the citrus fruits make interesting strongly flavored sweets. I save the peel in the refrigerator for a few days and make a batch of mixed peel. Keep the pith on, as it is transformed by the double boiling and is wonderful to eat. Retain syrup as an ice-cream topping.

Peel of 3 oranges, 3 lemons and 1 grapefruit
3   *cups granulated sugar*
3   *cups water*
1   *teaspoon baking soda*

Day 1: Wash the peel to remove the wax, and remove any pulp. Cut into quarters, or eighths or more if it is large fruit. Be conscious of cutting a neat shape. Dissolve the baking soda in boiling water and soak the peel for 20 minutes.

Drain and rinse the peel in cold water. Cook in fresh water until the peel is tender. Drain. Put 2 cups sugar and 3 cups water in the saucepan. Stir until the sugar dissolves and it is clear. Remove from heat and put in the peel. Leave for 2 days.

This candied peel has a great depth of flavor. It takes better than any candy you could buy.

Day 3: Remove the peel and add a cup of sugar to the syrup. Dissolve the sugar and bring to a boil. Drop in the peel and simmer until the peel is almost transparent.

Drain the peel on racks sitting in baking sheets. Reserve the syrup. Put the peel into a very slow oven to dry. On a very hot day, the peel could be dried outside, but beware of insects.

Day 5: Bring the syrup to a boil again and dip the peel into it. Drain again and dry. Store in airtight jars.

Glacé Dates

You'll need to have good quality dates for these stuffed delicacies.

3	tablespoons slivered almonds
1	tablespoon orange juice
	Confectioners' sugar as needed
1 1/2	cups dates, pitted
1 1/2	cups granulated sugar
1	cup water
1	teaspoon lemon juice

Make a stuffing of the almonds, orange juice and confectioners' sugar. Keep adding the confectioners' sugar until the mixture is firm. Stuff into the dates.

Make a syrup by putting the granulated sugar, water and lemon juice in a saucepan and cooking until you can put a spoon into the syrup and then into a glass of cold water and the surface of the spoon becomes like a layer of glass; it is then ready. Using a fine skewer, dip each date into the syrup and place on a greased baking sheet. When the dates are all completely dry, put them into small paper cases. Layer in an airtight tin.

Fruit and nut fudge placed in an attractive box makes a lovely, thoughtful Christmas present.

Candied Sweet Potatoes

A delicious alternative to potato chips. You could take them as a gift for your hosts at a Thanksgiving dinner.

2	pounds sweet potatoes
3	tablespoons butter
	Juice of half a lemon
4	tablespoons brandy
2	tablespoons brown sugar

Boil sweet potatoes until they are just cooked. Peel and slice them. Place the slices on greased baking sheets.

Melt the butter, remove from the heat and add lemon juice and brandy. Brush each slice and sprinkle the sugar over. Cook in a preheated oven at 375°F basting every 15 minutes. They take about 45 minutes to cook.

Fruit & Nut Fudge

1	cup raisins
1	cup dates, pitted
1	cup dried figs
1/2	cup dried apricots
1	cup cashew nuts
3	tablespoons orange juice

Chop the fruits and nuts as finely as possible. Combine in a bowl with the orange juice. Make them into balls and place each one in a paper case. Store in an airtight tin in layers with waxed paper between each layer.

VARIATION: Use less orange juice and a dash of brandy or rum.

 COOK'S NOTES: Homemade sweets are very cheap to make and generally much healthier if eaten in moderation. Remember to be patient and allow yourself plenty of time for all the moulding and dipping required for presenting them attractively.

Chocolate & Fruit Fudge

Rich and scrumptious, boxes of fudge are very well received as gifts. You could never buy anything so good.

1	tablespoon chopped dried pears
1	tablespoon chopped candied peel
2	tablespoons raisins
1	cup walnut pieces
2	tablespoons slivered almonds
1	cup dark chocolate melted
1	tablespoon confectioners' sugar
2	tablespoons brandy

Chop the fruit and nuts in a food processor. Put them into a bowl with the chocolate and confectioners' sugar and mix the paste. Add brandy until it becomes soft and pliable. Mould the fudge into balls and then roll them in confectioners' sugar. Put the balls of fudge into small paper cases and keep them in an airtight tin.

Apricot Sweetmeats

A simple sweet, delicious with after-dinner coffee or as a treat on its own.

1	cup dried apricots
2	tablespoons confectioners' sugar
	Whole almonds

Chop up the apricots in a food processor. Mix the apricot paste with the confectioners' sugar and a little water until you get a firm mixture. Roll into small balls and sprinkle with confectioners' sugar. Place an almond on each one.

VARIATION: Using a fine skewer, dip the balls in hot melted chocolate and place them on a greased baking sheet. Store in small paper cases in an airtight tin.

Toffees

A great stand-by for fund-raising events and for children's parties. Very easy to make, but great care must be taken handling the hot toffee syrup. It can cause shocking burns if spilt on the skin. Handle with care at setting and ladling stage.

2	pounds granulated sugar
1	cup water
1	tablespoon vinegar
1/4	teaspoon tartrate baking powder

Put all the ingredients in a large saucepan over a low heat. Stir until the sugar is dissolved. Cover with the lid for 2 minutes to prevent any sugar crystallizing on the side of the saucepan.

Remove the lid and boil rapidly until the syrup reaches 300°F. It takes about 15 minutes. The syrup turns a golden caramel color. Test by dipping half a teaspoonful into cold water for a moment or two; if it makes brittle shreds, it is ready. Be extremely careful so as to avoid burns from the hot toffee syrup. Ladle into paper cases, three-quarters filled. Sprinkle with coconut, or place an almond on the top of each.

VARIATIONS:
TOFFEE BRAZIL NUTS: When making toffees, save some of the syrup to coat some brazil nuts. Have a cup of brazil nuts ready and a greased baking sheet. Impale the nut on a needle and carefully dip it into the hot toffee. Hold the nut above the syrup until it stops dripping, then push it off the needle onto the baking sheet. Store in screw-top jars.

PINE NUT BRITTLE: Follow the recipe for toffee and add 3 cups of pine nuts after the toffee reaches its correct temperature. Pour the mixture onto greased baking sheets. Let it stand until it is hard. Break the brittle into pieces and store in a sterilized jar.

Old-fashioned toffees and toffee apples are great for children's parties and fund raising events. Put red coloring in the toffee mixture if you want the apples to look red.

TOFFEE APPLES: Old-fashioned toffee apples can be made with this toffee syrup. Put a wooden skewer into each fresh red apple and dip the apple into the toffee syrup. Place on greased baking sheet. Makes 20 apples.

Date & Walnut Nougat

This nougat lasts for ages. Store in a cool, dark place. It is very rich and filling, delightful with coffee at any time of the day.

1 1/2   cups dates, pitted
1   cup walnuts
3/4   cup pistachio nuts
1/2   cup superfine sugar
1/4   cup water
         Juice of half a lemon
         Walnut oil
         Confectioners' sugar
         Rice paper

Chop the dates and nuts finely in a food processor. Put the sugar and water in a saucepan and bring to a boil. When it first reaches golden brown, before the setting stage, remove from heat. Add the lemon juice, dates and nuts.

Put back on a low heat and cook for 10 minutes, stirring, then remove from the heat. When it is cool enough to handle, oil your hands and roll the mixture into logs. Leave them to harden, then roll them in confectioners' sugar. Store in layers between sheets of rice paper.

Coconut Chocolate

1   pound dark chocolate
1   cup desiccated coconut
1/4 teaspoon cinnamon

Melt the chocolate in a bowl by placing it in a saucepan of boiling water. Add the coconut and cinnamon and stir well. Pour into small paper cases. Sprinkle a little extra coconut on top. Store in layers in a tin.

Hazelnut Chocolate

1   pound milk chocolate
1   cup hazelnuts

Melt the chocolate in a bowl placed in boiling water. Grind half the hazelnuts in a food processor and mix into the chocolate. Add the whole hazelnuts and stir well. When the chocolate is cool enough to handle, shape into logs, then put into individual paper cases. Store in an airtight container.

Coconut Ice

A perennial favorite for presents and fund-raising events. Coconut ice looks very nice in cellophane packets tied with pastel ribbon.

2   pounds granulated sugar
1/2   cup milk
1   tablespoon butter
1 1/2 cups desiccated coconut
       Pink food coloring

Combine the sugar, milk and butter in a heavy saucepan and bring slowly to a boil. Stir occasionally. Boil for 5 minutes, stirring all the time.

Remove from heat; add the coconut. Mix well and pour half into a greased pan 1 inch deep. Put the pink coloring into the other half and pour into a separate pan. It sets quickly, so keep an eye on it for the next two steps.

When it is partly set, mark it into fingers. Cut when it is cool.

Marshmallows

1 1/2 cups vanilla superfine sugar
1/2   cup cold water
4   teaspoons gelatin
1/2   cup hot water
1/2   cup desiccated coconut toasted

Put the sugar and cold water into a bowl and beat with an electric mixer for 4 minutes. Dissolve the gelatin in the hot water. Now add the gelatin to the sugar water and beat until it is thick. Pour into a pan 11 x 7½ x 1½ inches. When it is cool and firm, cut it into squares. Coat squares with the desiccated coconut. Store in an airtight jar or tin.

COOKIES

Easter Biscuits

These biscuits have been traditionally made and eaten at Easter time for hundreds of years. They make a delightful change from chocolate eggs as Easter gifts.

1	cup flour
1/2	teaspoon salt
1	teaspoon ground cinnamon
1	teaspoon ground ginger
1/4	cup butter
4	tablespoons superfine sugar
3	tablespoons currants
1	tablespoon chopped dried apricots
2	tablespoons milk
1	egg, beaten

Sift the flour, salt and spices. Rub in the butter until the mixture resembles bread crumbs. Mix in the sugar, currants and apricots. Make a well and pour in a little milk and the beaten egg. Keep mixing and adding milk until you have a stiff dough. Refrigerate for 2 hours.

Roll out the dough very thinly and cut into rounds. Put them on greased baking sheets in an oven preheated to 400°F. They will take about 20 minutes to bake. They are ready when they begin to change color.

Coconut Macaroons

I give macaroons away in pretty boxes with sheets of rice paper between layers.

2	egg whites
2	teaspoons cornstarch
4	tablespoons superfine sugar
5	tablespoons desiccated coconut
20	almonds

Beat the egg whites until they are frothy. Mix in the cornstarch and superfine sugar and then the coconut. With a teaspoon, measure out spoonfuls of the mixture and place them on a greased baking sheet. Put an almond on top of each, pressing down gently so that the top is slightly flattened. Bake in a preheated oven at 350°F for about 20 minutes. They should be firm and turn a golden color. Store in an airtight tin.

Valentine Cookies

Give your favorite friend some heart-shaped cookies on St Valentine's Day.

2	cups flour
1/2	teaspoon baking powder
3	tablespoons butter
1	cup vanilla sugar
1	egg
2	tablespoons rum
ICING	
1	egg white
1	cup confectioners' sugar
1/2	teaspoon lemon juice
	Red food coloring

Shortbread is a favorite with most people. It looks special made in the round with pinched edges.

Sift the flour and baking powder. Cream the butter, then add the sugar gradually until light and fluffy. Add the egg and rum. Then beat in the flour and baking powder, a little at a time. Refrigerate the dough for 2 hours.

Roll out the dough to 1/8 inch thick. Cut out the cookies with a heart-shaped cutter. Place on greased baking sheets and put in an oven preheated to 400°F. They will be ready in 10 minutes. Cool on wire racks.

To make the icing, beat the egg white and add the sugar gradually. Add the lemon juice and red coloring. When the cookies are cool, ice them with a palette knife or put the icing in a piping bag and pipe your friend's name onto the cookie.

Shortbread

This is a recipe for real Scottish shortbread, a welcome gift at any time. It takes a lot of kneading, but it is really worth while. It looks lovely wrapped in cellophane and tied with a tartan ribbon. If it goes soft, heat in a moderate oven for 10 to 15 minutes.

3/4	*cup butter*
1/4	*cup superfine sugar*
2	*cups flour*

Cream butter and then gradually add the sugar until the mixture is light and fluffy. Add the flour gradually. Now knead the dough for 15 minutes. It should be very smooth.

Roll out the dough into an 8 inch round.

Ginger Nuts

A favorite cookie of mine. We adored them as children and soon learnt to make them ourselves.

2   cups flour
2   teaspoon bicarbonate of soda
4   tablespoons brown sugar
1/4   cup butter
4   tablespoons light corn syrup
1   egg
2   teaspoons ground ginger
2   teaspoons ground cinnamon
15-20 almonds

Sift the flour and soda into a bowl; mix in the brown sugar. Melt the butter and light corn syrup and mix in with the dough. Add the egg and the spices. Roll out the dough and cut into rounds. Place an almond in the middle of each one. Put on greased baking sheets in a preheated oven at 400°F. They should be ready in 15 to 20 minutes. Cool on a wire rack.

Use a flan ring if you have one. Make sure the dough surface is smooth and even. Crimp the edges of the dough and prick the surface with a fork. Bake in a preheated oven at 300°F for 20 minutes. Reduce the temperature to 275°F and bake for 40 minutes. Cool on a wire rack.

Gingerbread Men

A perennial favorite with children and adults alike, gingerbread men are not very difficult to make and give much pleasure. Decorate the table with them, or decorate the Christmas tree. Use cut paper straws placed in the head before baking to make a hole for hanging. Make heart-shaped ginger cookie for St Valentine's Day with a heart-shaped cookie cutter.

1/4   cup butter
1/3   cup brown sugar
1/3   cup light corn syrup
3   cups flour
1   teaspoon ground ginger
1   teaspoon cinnamon
3   teaspoons baking soda
1   egg
2   teaspoons vanilla extract

Melt the butter, sugar and syrup over a very low heat, stirring occasionally. Allow to cool.

Sift the flour and spices into a bowl. Add the baking soda to the butter mixture. Make a well in the flour and add the butter mixture. Mix well and then add the egg and vanilla extract to make a soft dough. Roll out the dough to 1/8 inch thick. Cut out the gingerbread men with a cutter or a sharp knife. Add currants for the eyes and a slice of candied cherry for the mouth. Put them on a greased baking sheet in a preheated oven at 325°F for 10 minutes. Cool on a wire rack.

 COOK'S NOTES: Keep a permanent supply of vanilla sugar by putting 2 vanilla beans in a large jar and fill it up with sugar. Top up the sugar as you use it.

CAKES

Panettone

An Italian cake associated with Christmas, though we tend to eat it all year round panettone is really an enriched bread. If you like the panettone you have bought in the shops, wait until you taste this home made one! Just the pleasure of smelling it while cooking is almost enough to justify the time spent making it.

1/2	cup butter
1/2	cup sugar
2	egg yolks
2 3/4	cups flour
1	teaspoon tartrate baking powder
1	teaspoon baking soda
1	egg
1	cup milk warmed
3/4	cup golden raisins
1/2	cup candied lemon peel
	Peel of 1 lemon, grated

Cream the butter until it is fluffy. Add the sugar gradually and beat until it is creamy. Beat in an egg yolk. Sift the flour, baking powder and soda. Stir in some of the flour. Beat in the second yolk, then a little flour and then the whole egg. Beat in the warm milk. Beat in the remaining flour. Mix well for about 15 minutes. Stir the golden raisins, candied peel and grated rind into the batter. Pour into a greased and floured cake pan and bake in a preheated oven at 350°F for about 45 minutes. Let it cool in the tin for 10 minutes and then turn out on a wire rack. Sprinkle with confectioners' sugar.

Christmas Fruit & Nut Cake

A cake made almost entirely of fruit and nuts. It is very rich and has become so popular it may soon supplant the traditional Christmas cake. Cut thin slices when serving.

1	cup brazil nuts
1	cup walnuts
1	cup dates, pitted
1/2	cup prunes chopped
1/3	cup chopped candied peel
1/3	cup candied cherries
1/2	cup golden raisins
	Peel of 1 lemon, grated
1/2	cup brandy
3	tablespoons flour
1/2	teaspoon baking powder
1/2	cup brown sugar
3	eggs
1	teaspoon vanilla extract

Put the nuts, fruit and lemon peel into a bowl and pour in the brandy. Mix well, cover and leave to macerate for a week.

Sift the flour and baking powder together and mix with the fruit and nuts. Then add the sugar, eggs and vanilla and mix well. Put into a well-greased and floured oblong pan. Smooth the top, making sure there are some nuts on the top for decoration. Cover with foil.

Put into an oven preheated to 300°F and bake for 1 1/2 to 2 hours. Take the foil off for the last 30 minutes. Leave to cool for 10 minutes in the pan, then turn out on a wire rack. Store the cake in a tin with several layers of foil around the cake. Keep in a cool place. Once opened, refrigerate.

Orange & Almond Cake

This is a very simple cake to make and very delicious. A great contribution to a picnic lunch.

2	oranges
6	eggs
1	cup ground almonds
1	cup sugar
	Zest of 1 lemon
1	teaspoon baking powder
1 1/2	tablespoons slivered almonds

Scrub the oranges and boil them whole for 1 1/2 to 2 hours until they are very soft. When cool, cut them up roughly and take the seeds out. Pulp them in a food processor.

Beat the eggs and fold in all the other ingredients. Pour the batter into a buttered and floured cake pan and sprinkle the top with slivered almonds. Put into an oven preheated to 425°F for about an hour. Leave to cool in the tin for 10 minutes before turning out on a wire rack.

Walnut Cake

A French-style cake to eat as a dessert.

1	cup walnuts
5	egg whites
1 1/2	cups superfine sugar
1/2	cup apricot jam

Grind the walnuts in a food processor. Beat the egg whites until they are stiff. Gradually add the sugar, then the walnuts. Divide the mixture in half and make two 7 inch rounds. Use a flan ring if you have one. Put onto a well-greased and floured baking sheet. Bake in a preheated oven at 350°F for 10 minutes.

When cool, spread the apricot jam over one layer and place the other on top. Sprinkle the top with confectioners' sugar.

 COOK'S NOTES: *Double grease a cake pan or pudding basin to be sure of success in turning out the cake or pudding. Brush melted butter over the surface. Put in the refrigerator for 10 minutes, then grease again and refrigerate. Sprinkle in a little flour just before pouring the mixture in.*

FRUIT DESSERTS

Prunes in Brandy

A yummy dessert to make on the spur of the moment if you are industrious enough to have a kitchen cabinet full of goodies like this. Serve the prunes with vanilla ice-cream, the liqueur poured over as a sauce. The coconut macaroons on page 39 would make a perfect accompaniment. The liqueur is excellent to sip with coffee.

So simple to prepare, prunes in brandy make a wonderful ending to a formal dinner.

1	pound prunes
1	stick cinnamon
3	cloves
	Peel of half an orange
1	cup superfine sugar
1/2	cup water
1/2	bottle brandy

Fill a sterilized wide-necked bottle with prunes. They should fill three-quarters of the bottle. Tuck in cinnamon, cloves and peel amongst the fruit. Make a sugar syrup by heating the sugar and water. Let it cool and pour over the fruit. Top the bottle up with brandy. Seal and label. Keep for 2 months before opening.

Plum Pudding

This is very simple to make and a 'no failure' family recipe. We make large quantities and fill up different sized basins for giving away or eating on different occasions. They last for a year in the refrigerator. This recipe is half our usual one. When giving a plum pudding away as a present, wrap the basin in calico and tie with red and green ribbon. Attach instructions for reheating and the sauce recipe (page 22).

1	pound golden raisins
1	cup raisins
1	cup prunes, pitted
1/2	cup dates, pitted
1/2	cup currants
2	tablespoons chopped candied peel
1	cooking apple, peeled and grated
1	tablespoon grated lemon peel
1	cup brandy
1/3	cup butter
3/4	cup brown sugar
3	eggs
3	cups day-old bread crumbs
2	tablespoons flour
1/2	teaspoon ground allspice berries
1/2	teaspoon grated nutmeg
1/2	teaspoon ground cinnamon
1/2	teaspoon baking soda
1/2	teaspoon salt

Chop up all the dried fruits and mixed peel, and place in a large bowl. Add the apple, lemon peel and brandy. Mix well, cover and leave for a week.

Beat the butter until fluffy: add the sugar and beat until the mixture is creamy. Add the eggs one at a time, beating well in between. Combine the cream mixture with the fruit and bread crumbs. Sift the flour, spices, soda and salt and add to the cake mixture.

Double grease heatproof basins by melting a little butter and brushing it over the entire surface of the basin, refrigerating for 10 minutes and greasing again. This will ensure the pudding will turn out perfectly. Transfer the cake mixture into the individual basins.

Cover the top of each basin with 2 layers of kitchen foil and tie with string. Place in a saucepan with boiling water halfway up the side of the basin. Steam for 6 hours. Check the water level in case you have to replace some. Keep the foil cover on and store in the refrigerator. On Christmas Day, reheat in the same way for 2 hours.

Cherries in Brandy

I never know which is best, the fruit or the liqueur. So simply made and so nice to receive as a present.

3	pounds dark cherries, underripe
2/3	cup granulated sugar
1/2	cup water
1	cinnamon stick
1/2	bottle brandy

Wash the cherries and trim the stalks to within 3/4 inch of the fruit. Prick over cherries with a needle and put them in a wide-necked, sterilized jar.

Put the sugar, water and cinnamon stick into a saucepan, dissolve the sugar and simmer for 5 minutes. Pour over the cherries. Now pour the brandy over the cherries and fill up the jar. Seal and store in a cool place for at least a month before opening.

FRUIT LIQUEUR'S

Strawberry Gin

This lovely pale pink liqueur is a very special gift for any time of the year and any occasion. It can be sipped or used as a flavoring for strawberry desserts.

4   cups strawberries
1 1/2 cups superfine sugar
½ to 1 bottle gin

Clean and hull the strawberries and pack into a wide-necked sterilized jar. Pour sugar over and then top the bottle up with gin. Store for 1 to 2 months or until strawberries lose their color.
  Strain liquid through cheesecloth and pour into a sterilized bottle and store for a month.

Passionfruit Liqueur

This can be drunk as an aperitif or spooned over ice-cream or yogurt.

2   cups passionfruit pulp
1   cup brown sugar
1   quart white rum

Put the passionfruit in a sterilized jar. Make the syrup by putting the sugar and rum in a saucepan over a low heat and dissolving the sugar. Do not let it come to a boil. Pour the syrup over the fruit and seal. Do not open for at least 2 months.

Pineapple Liqueur

There are few fruits that don't produce a good liqueur. Keep this one for at least 2 months before opening and you will certainly be rewarded.

1   pineapple, peeled and finely sliced
1 1/2 cups superfine sugar
1/2 bottle brandy

Choose a jar that will contain the pineapple, layer on layer, with about 1 inch left at the top. Put the fruit in a sterilized jar, following the original shape of the pineapple, and add the sugar. Cover well with brandy, making sure there are no air bubbles. Seal, label and store.

Orange Liqueur

I always use cheap brandy. It is nice to think when making these liqueur's that you actually end up with twice the original amount plus a delicious dessert fruit to eat with yogurt or ice-cream.

4   oranges
2   cups superfine sugar
1   cup water
1/2 bottle brandy

Cut oranges in half and squeeze out the juice; retain. Cut the peel into bite-sized pieces and remove any pith. Make a sugar syrup by dissolving the sugar, orange juice and water then simmering for 15 minutes. Put peel into wide-necked sterilized jars and pour the syrup over. Top the bottles up with the brandy. Seal, label and store for 2 months.

Quince Vodka

Quince vodka is a delicate pale color and makes an excellent aperitif. The whole of the quince is used to macerate in the sugar and vodka for months and then strained to make a clear liqueur.

2   quinces
1   cup superfine sugar
½ to 1 bottle vodka

Orange peel and sugar syrup transform cheap brandy into nectar fit for the gods. This orange liqueur is one of my favorite fruit liqueur's. A beautiful ending to a rich dinner.

Use ripe yellow quinces. Wash and remove the fluff. Remove the stalks and cores but not the skin. Cut into small pieces. Put them into a wide-necked sterilized jar. Pour the sugar over and top the bottle up with vodka. Seal and store for 4 months. (You could try it after 3 months; it is up to individual tastes.) strain the liqueur off into a sterilized bottle and seal.

INDEX

Page numbers in **bold** type indicate illustrations.